A journey *of* love

REACHING OUT AS JESUS DID

A journey *of* love

REACHING OUT AS JESUS DID

Kate Hayes

A journey of love: reaching out as Jesus did

An individual or small group Bible resource from Scripture Union

Scripture Union, 207-209 Queensway, Bletchley, MK2 2EB, England, UK
Email: info@scriptureunion.org.uk
Website: www.scriptureunion.org.uk

ISBN: 1 84427 232 X
    978 1 84427 232 7

Scripture Union Australia
Locked Bag 2, Central Coast Business Centre, NSW 2252
www.su.org.au

First published in the U.K. by Scripture Union, 2006

Scripture taken from the New Living Translation, British text, published by Tyndale House Publishers, Inc., Wheaton, Illinois, USA, and distributed by STL Ltd., Carlisle, Cumbria, England.

British Library Cataloguing-in-Publication data
A catalogue record for this book is available from the British Library.

Cover design: Philip Grundy
Internal design and typesetting by Servis Filmsetting Ltd., Manchester

Printed in Great Britain by Henry Ling Limited, at the Dorset Press, Dorchester, DT1 1HD

꒜ Scripture Union is an international Christian charity working with churches in more than 130 countries, providing resources to bring the good news about Jesus Christ to children, young people and families and to encourage them to develop spiritually through the Bible and prayer.
As well as our network of volunteers, staff and associates who run holidays, church-based events and school Christian groups, we produce a wide range of publications and support those who use our resources through training programmes.

The Way Ahead

*T*his book is for anyone, as an individual or with a small group, who wants to grow in their understanding of the journey of love for others that all followers of Jesus are called to take. This journey of love seeks to share the good news of Jesus with the world around us, not as an act of duty or one taken out of fear, but as a response to the love God has already shown to us.

In our society people now hold a vast array of different beliefs about life and eternity. Where once most would have known the story of God and man as described in the Bible, today many do not in any detail. People's opinions of the Church and Christians seem to be formed less through personal experience and more through the impressions they gain from the media; impressions that are often negative, deserved or not. For many the Church is seen as boring and irrelevant, and so its message of love, hope and transformation goes unheard.

However this inability to communicate our good news to others effectively can't all be put down to poor publicity. The Church itself is often slow to share its good news in a way 'outsiders' will understand and can be reluctant to welcome them in. Perhaps sometimes we are put off because people don't seem interested or ignore the claims of Jesus, seeing them as just one alternative amongst many paths to spiritual enlightenment. As individual Christians we may fear that we will do it all wrong or maybe just don't know where to start. Even the ordinary demands of our own lives can get in the way of following the call of Jesus to 'go and make disciples of all the world' (Matthew 28:19).

So, just how can we share this good news with this apparently uninterested world? Why should we bother anyway? What difference does this call make to the way I live or the way my church goes about its activities? What does it mean to share Jesus and make disciples? In this series we explore these questions and others like them and see what help and hope the Bible has to offer. Our goal is to see ourselves and others come into a life-changing relationship with Jesus.

The Solitary Traveller

This book is a companion for the solitary traveller. You can work through the material at your own pace, ignoring only those sections marked with the group logo. It may be helpful for you to record your thoughts along the way, either on the pages or in a separate notebook.

The Group of Travellers

This book is also a companion for the small group. You may have come together with a Christian friend, as a prayer triplet, as an existing small fellowship group or you may be part of a group specially convened for Lent or some other season of the year. Decide whether one person will lead each time you meet, or whether a different person will lead each session. You may want to skip those sections marked with the solitary traveller logo.

Using the Material

The material is divided into six sessions or chapters and there is a consistent pattern to the material in each.

Setting Out will ease you gently into the focus of the session through some fun questions or activities. Don't skip this part, even if you are a solitary traveller, because however light this material seems it will flag up some important attitudes and preconceptions and will prepare you for deeper exploration of some key issues. Within the group setting, this opening time will develop relationships and encourage honest sharing which will ultimately help the group to be more comfortable in praying together.

Signposts will take you into the Bible. This time of discovery alone or together will open up a number of lines of thought as you follow through the questions. For groups, this section will particularly encourage discussion and the sharing of experiences.

Prayer is the next section, during which time there is opportunity to pray in a way that relates to the focus of the session so far. Don't be tempted to rush this; it is just as important as the rest of the session.

Finally, there is a **Further Afield** section. This allows further exploration of related issues in the Bible. Depending on how long you have together, groups wanting to lengthen the Bible study section could use some or all of this material in the **Signposts** section. If time is limited, group members might like to use **Further Afield** at home for personal study during the week. Individuals can choose to use some or all of this section.

About the Author

Kate Hayes became a Christian aged 12 after being 'dragged along' to a Pathfinder meeting by a friend. After studying Psychology at university, she did teacher training but then changed direction, working in bookshops and in software testing for the book trade. Since 1994 her family have been in Dukinfield, Greater Manchester, where she co-ordinates and writes materials for small groups at St John's Church.

1 God's Mission

Y ou're delighted that after all that time and effort, you have made something truly wonderful. Hours pass as you admire it from every angle and drag in friends to see how well it turned out. Then, suddenly, something happens and the signs of damage spread across it. You've poured love and energy into it but now it's no longer as you had planned and hoped. Sadness overcomes your initial delight until you realise it is possible to overcome this, to rebuild it and make it perfect once again. Would you bother to start that process of re-creation or would you scrap it?

The world was damaged by the choices of God's beloved children, but he had already prepared a rescue plan that would renew his creation.

Setting Out

1 You've been invited to a fancy dress party. Do you:

    a Come up with an idea, get out the sewing machine, the stapler and the glue stick and get it made;

    b End up without an outfit at all – you've spent all your time putting together ideas for everyone else;

    c Come up with ten ideas, all hopeless, and get a friend to lend you something instead;

    d Spend a fortune to rent an outfit which someone more talented could have made for almost nothing;

    e Grab a bin liner out of the cupboard at the last minute and go as a punk rocker, again;

    f Pretend you never received the invite or feign illness on the day and stay at home?

2 You're at home alone, and there's nothing urgently requiring your attention. Do you:

    a Take the opportunity to clean out your cupboards;

    b Start that book you've been meaning to read for ages;

    c Get out your paints, embroidery or tools and spend the time making something;

    d Sleep;

    e Panic – it's too quiet – and go out?

3 You're making tea and you've got four visitors joining you. You've got all afternoon free. Do you:

a Buy some posh ready meals and spend the afternoon tarting them up to look homemade;

b Spend a few minutes throwing together some pasta and sauce and do something interesting for the rest of the afternoon;

c Ring round your visitors and get them to bring a course each;

d See it as a great opportunity to try out that new recipe book you got for Christmas – if it doesn't work you can always fetch a takeaway;

e Go to town and create a 'dining experience' they'll never forget: themed food, table decorations, atmosphere, outfit . . . the lot?

4 When you think about it, the last time you made something (anything) just because you wanted to was:

a Today;

b This month;

c This week;

d This year;

e Sometime since you left school but not recently;

f Before you started school ?

5 Do you see yourself as someone who enjoys making things? Did your answers reflect that?

6 What is your favourite (or least disliked) form of creative activity?

Signposts

IN THE BEGINNING

Read Genesis 1.

1 How did God feel about his creation?

2 Do you think creation reflects his character in some way? If so, how?

In the beginning, everything about creation was 'excellent' (Genesis 1:31).
Then, Adam and Eve chose to follow their own desires rather than obeying God

and in doing so their close relationship with him was broken. Sin marred God's perfect creation, but instead of abandoning what he had made he chose to reach out and restore it to relationship with him.

THE RESCUE PLAN

1 Read Genesis 12:1–6.

1 What did God say he would do for Abraham?

2 What did Abraham have to do in return?

3 Do you think this was a pretty simple task for Abraham or not? Why?

With hindsight we know God kept his promise to Abraham; but Abraham himself had to live by faith, seeing only hints that God had really meant what he said.

In time, God's covenant promises with Abraham are renewed with the whole nation of Israel (Exodus 19:3–6). Unfortunately, just like Adam and Eve, Israel often chose to follow their own desires. Instead of pointing other nations to God they ended up living just like everybody else (2 Kings 17:15).

It might seem that God's plan to restore creation was floundering, but then Jesus, man and God in one person, came to complete the mission. He gave everyone a second chance to live in relationship with God.

2 Read John 1:1–18.

Abraham was called to obey God, so that he might father the nation who would be God's people. Israel was called to live in obedient relationship with God and point other nations to him.

1 What part is Jesus to play in God's mission?

2 Why is that such good news for us today?

CALLED

1 You're sitting quietly reflecting on life when the phone rings. Someone very important announces that you have been chosen to be a British ambassador abroad. In fact, they are so keen to have you that you can choose any country in the world to go to. Where would you choose and why?

2 You put down the phone and head off to start packing. How are you feeling about what lies ahead? Are you thrilled and excited? Apprehensive? Something else?

3 Your new role as ambassador means you are representing this country abroad. What national qualities and characteristics do you think our ambassadors should demonstrate? Are there some that should be avoided?

4 Why would it matter what an ambassador's character is like?

Read 2 Corinthians 5:18–20.

1 God called Paul to be an ambassador, sharing the good news of Jesus with others. We may not have Paul's specific gifts or calling, but all of us who follow Jesus are called to be witnesses – ambassadors – for him. What responsibilities does that role have?

2 Do you think it is possible for someone to be an ambassador for Christ if they don't know Jesus for themselves? Why?

3 Do you know Jesus for yourself? Or is this something you're still thinking about?

4 If you do know Jesus, what has made that a good thing for you? Why should someone else follow him too?

5 How do you feel about being Jesus' ambassador? Is this more exciting than being an ambassador for your country? Or more scary? Why do you think you feel this way?

God reached out to his creation seeking to connect with us. Through Abraham and Israel he demonstrated the kind of relationship he wants with us and then in Jesus made that relationship possible. Now the task of continuing God's mission passes to all those who live in relationship with him, all those who follow Jesus. We are to point others to Jesus and show what life with him is like.

Prayer

If a shepherd has one hundred sheep, and one wanders away and is lost, what will he do? Won't he leave the ninety-nine others and go out into the hills to search for the lost one? Matthew 18:12

People often speak of searching for truth or searching for God. The Bible shows us that whilst we need to be ready, really it is God who is reaching out to us.

Begin in silence.

Look back to a time when God was reaching out to you, perhaps before you decided to follow him, perhaps a time when you felt very distant from him. How did God reach out to you then? Maybe it was through other people, his Word, events in your life or even things you read or watched.

In your heart, thank him that he sought you out and for his enduring love for you.

End this section with one person reading these verses or by all reading them together:

Your unfailing love, O LORD, is as vast as the heavens;

your faithfulness reaches beyond the clouds.

Your righteousness is like the mighty mountains,

your justice like the ocean depths.

You care for people and animals alike, O LORD.

How precious is your unfailing love, O God!

All humanity finds shelter

in the shadow of your wings.

You feed them from the abundance of your own house,

letting them drink from your rivers of delight.

Psalm 36:5–8

Continue by thinking about people you know who don't yet have that relationship with God. Bring their names to God now. You might like to say their names aloud, or to spend a few moments in silent prayer.

Continue to pray for these people this week. Pray that God would reveal himself to them, and that if God wants you to help that process, he would show you what to do.

Further Afield

1 HERE I AM

Read 1 Samuel 3:1–21.

1 If you were dozing off and heard someone call your name how would you react? Perhaps your answer depends on whether you live alone or not. When this happened to Samuel he assumed it was Eli, the only other person nearby, who was calling him. Imagine you're Samuel. It's late and you're tired. How would you want to respond to this voice?

2 Three times Samuel hears the voice and goes to Eli, to find it wasn't Eli at all. Why do you think Samuel didn't just ignore the voice after the first couple of times?

3 Samuel finds the real source of the voice, listens and obeys the Lord. How does God respond to Samuel's willingness and obedience?

4 Sometimes God speaks at a time when we'd rather be doing something else or asks us to do things we find difficult. Are we ready to listen to him speak to us, even if what he wants to say is difficult to hear?

5 Give God an opportunity to speak to you now. Spend a few minutes silently focused on him.

2 PASSING IT ON

Read 2 Corinthians 4:5,6.

1 Imagine you're at work when the phone rings. Someone wants to leave a message for one of your colleagues. Do you:

    a Refuse to take it – you know they never look at their messages;
    b Write it down for them;
    c Listen carefully knowing you'll remember to pass it on;
    d Half listen, make a note of the number then lose the note and rapidly forget anyone even rang?

2 God gave Samuel a message to pass on. Like Samuel we have a message to share, but our message is not just a set of words but the promise of a relationship with Jesus. How do we go about sharing that message with others?

Pray that God will help you live out his message, the good news of Jesus, in your life today.

3 COMPLETING THE TASK

Read Romans 12:4,5 and 1 Peter 4:10,11.

One day at work your struggling company decides to save money by getting everyone to take a turn at cleaning the building. After much grumbling agreement is reached and each section of the company takes turns to do the job. Your day comes. You and John turn up with a brush and dustpan and set to work cleaning floors. James helps you very half-heartedly. Thomas does everything else by himself and Mary says she's hopeless at cleaning and goes home instead.

1 How successfully has your section completed their cleaning responsibilities?

2 How do you feel about Mary?

3 What would have helped your section complete the task properly?

God's mission to bring people to know Jesus isn't the same as cleaning a building, but still works best when everyone plays their part well. In these passages Peter and Paul remind us that:

- God has given everybody a gift to use in his service (1 Peter 4:10);
- We are all needed (Romans 12:5);
- We are to serve God wherever we find ourselves to the very best of our ability (1 Peter 4:10,11).

In sharing the message of Jesus with the world around us we all have a different part to play.

Ask yourself:

- Am I willing to play my part in this?
- Do I really serve God, at work, in church, in my relationships, to the best of my ability?

Ask God to show you if there is something you could do or change so you can serve him more effectively.

2 One Way

As you're watching TV, someone claims they know how to get rid of wrinkles or has found the best place to eat in Britain or knows who is the greatest footballer ever. Do you respond with a degree of suspicion? Too often we hear such comments but find it doesn't work for us, or we don't agree. We might give their technique to reduce wrinkles a try, visit the restaurant or watch the player, but if our wrinkles remain unchanged or our tastebuds unimpressed we won't agree they were right. Sometimes we may not even want to agree. After all half the fun of sport seems to be in arguing about who is really the greatest ever. In the end we tend to trust our own experiences more than we trust the claims of others, an attitude that can include spiritual things too.

Setting Out

1 You are to spend a month on a desert island. Unfortunately, unlike those cast away by Radio Four, you are only allowed to take three pieces of music with you. Which three will you choose and why?

2 Of people aged 12 to 74, 51% bought at least one music album in 2002 (Office for National Statistics, Social Trends 34). However old you are, when did you last buy a music album and what was it?

3 If you could choose to hear any one live musical performance from any era in history – from JS Bach playing his own music to the Beatles performing at The Cavern – who would you go and listen to?

Whether we love the music of Perry Como, the Arctic Monkeys, Charles Wesley or Chopin, some people will agree with us and others won't. Musical preferences can arouse strong feelings and trigger passionate discussions, but in the end most of us accept people's different musical tastes. Similarly we probably agree that someone can choose to spend their free time doing embroidery or bird-watching or cooking or skateboarding or playing cricket, even when *we* can't understand why. Sometimes lyrics of some forms of music might be seen as questionable, some hobbies less than wholesome, but on the whole we accept that everyone is different and that's fine.

Many people believe that spirituality and religious belief have now become matters of choice in the same way as music and hobbies. If it works for you it doesn't matter whether you are an atheist or a Christian, believe in astrology or put together your own mix and match set of beliefs. We don't expect everyone to like the same music or enjoy the same hobby and so we don't expect everyone to hold the same religious beliefs, we are different and that's fine.

4   Do you think that reflects current attitudes to religion and spirituality?

5   What do you think people are looking for from their religious and spiritual beliefs?

6   Why do you think many people avoid conventional religious beliefs and choose their own spiritual paths?

7   Assuming you have made the choice to follow Jesus, were you interested in other forms of religious belief before that happened?

8   Why do you follow Jesus rather than any other kind of religious or spiritual belief?

Signposts

WHO IS JESUS?

Read John 6:47–58 and 14:1–11.

These are just two of the times John records Jesus' claims about himself.

1   How does Jesus describe himself in these two passages?

2   What does he say are the benefits of believing him?

3 How do Jesus' claims differ from those who say you can find God by following *their* teachings?

CS Lewis is well known for saying that any ordinary man making statements like these 'would either be a lunatic – on the level with the man who says he is a poached egg – or else he would be the Devil of Hell' (*Mere Christianity*, Fount). These statements only make sense if Jesus really is God himself.

Read John 6:60–69.

1 How did people react to the things Jesus said about himself?

2 Why do you think they responded in this way?

3 What about today? Imagine Jesus said these things on a chat show. How do you think people would react?

SHARING OUR GOOD NEWS

Read 1 Peter 3:15–17.

1 We live in a country where people hold many different religious beliefs. If we talk about these claims of Jesus some people will see it as arrogant or be upset by it. Should we keep quiet and avoid upsetting other people?

2 If not, how can we share the good news of Jesus whilst showing respect and love for those who disagree?

3 A friend has never heard your favourite kind of music. Which of these will demonstrate just how good it is:
   a Give them the sheet music for your favourite piece;
   b Show them statistics which tell them how many people go to concerts and buy this kind of music;
   c Get out your CDs and persuade them to listen to some;
   d Show them pictures of people who play the music and your old concert ticket stubs;

e Describe the musical style in detail;

f Take them to a live concert?

4 Why did you choose that answer?

5 Why might just telling them how great it is be unconvincing?

As followers of Jesus we believe he is the only source of truth and life for everyone. However we are just one of many voices saying we know the truth. We need to show Jesus through the way we live so that people will want to meet him for themselves.

UNDER OBSERVATION

Read 2 Corinthians 6:3–10.

In *The Message*, verse 4 says, 'Our work as God's servants gets validated – or not – in the details. People are watching us as we stay at our post, alertly, unswervingly . . .'

1 Have you ever had someone say to you 'I didn't think Christians were supposed to do that. . .'?

2 Why do people care how Christians behave?

3 If our lives are to reflect Jesus to others, what qualities should we display?

4 Be honest with yourself. If someone looks at you, what qualities do they really see?

5 How would someone else answer this question for you?

6 How does your answer change if you think about yourself in different situations: at home; out with friends; at church; at work?

7 If there is a mismatch between what we're like and what Jesus wants us to be like what could help us change?

If there is area where you are struggling to behave as Jesus would want, perhaps in a difficult relationship or in the complex demands of your working life, why not share that with your group and ask them to pray for you.

Prayer

Read these verses from Ephesians 2:1–10, one section at a time. Between sections there are suggestions for reflection that could be used in silence or to guide open prayer.

Once you were dead, doomed forever because of your many sins. You used to live just like the rest of the world, full of sin, obeying Satan, the mighty prince of the power of the air. He is the spirit at work in the hearts of those who refuse to obey God. All of us used to live that way, following the passions and desires of our evil nature. We were born with an evil nature, and we were under God's anger just like everyone else.

Think again about people in your life who don't yet know Jesus. Pray that the way you live might encourage them to want to know more about him.

But God is so rich in mercy, and he loved us so very much, that even while we were dead because of our sins, he gave us life when he raised Christ from the dead. (It is only by God's special favour that you have been saved!) For he raised us from the dead along with Christ, and we are seated with him in the heavenly realms – all because we are one with Christ Jesus. And so God can always point to us as examples of the incredible wealth of his favour and kindness toward us, as shown in all he has done for us through Christ Jesus.

Thank God for this amazing gift of life that he has given you because of Jesus.

Q: What else could you thank him for this week?

God saved you by his special favor when you believed. And you can't take credit for this; it is a gift from God. Salvation is not a reward for the good things we have done, so none of us can boast about it. For we are God's masterpiece.

He has created us anew in Christ Jesus, so that we can do the good things he planned for us long ago.

God created us to do good things. What is he calling you to do? Do these things seem small and insignificant? Remember that everything we do can show others what Jesus is really like.

If you are meeting as a group, end by each sharing one name of someone who doesn't yet know Jesus. Pray together for these people over the remaining weeks of the course. Pray for their ordinary needs and for opportunities to share Jesus with them.

Further Afield

1 I AM THE BREAD OF LIFE: JOHN 6:29–40

Food, glorious food. Is that how you feel? For some whatever it is, if you can eat it it's great. Others are more fussy or happy to stick with their familiar choices. Even in places where food is in short supply everyone needs regular food to be healthy. Here in the same way we see that a regular intake of Jesus is essential for us to thrive spiritually.

1   How often do you put aside time to eat physical food?

2   How often do you put aside time to spend alone with Jesus?

3   Do we see spending time with Jesus as essential as eating or is it something we are happy to discard when time is short or enthusiasm low?

4   Why might it be so good for us to make this time with him a regular habit?

2 I AM THE LIGHT OF THE WORLD: JOHN 8:12

When blackout regulations were introduced in 1939 they were so effective that many people were killed and injured because they couldn't see where they were going or be seen by others. Even though the regulations changed so people could carry a dimmed torch, batteries were so scarce that it made little difference. Here we are reminded that we can get just as lost and confused spiritually as someone trying to move around in total darkness. If we want our lives to go in the right direction, we need to keep our eyes on the light, on Jesus himself.

Spend some time reflecting on what it means that Jesus is the light of the world.

You could read John 1:1–9, or perhaps light a candle and use that to focus your thoughts.

Q: How has he brought light to your life? Do you sometimes take your eyes off the light and find yourself stumbling around in the dark? How could you keep yourself focused more closely on Jesus, the light of the world?

3 I AM THE GOOD SHEPHERD: JOHN 10:1–30

You answer the phone to be greeted with enthusiasm by the person on the other end. They launch into a conversation with you asking about all kinds of things in your life. There's just one problem, you've just no idea who it is. Desperately you start fishing for clues hoping they won't guess before you identify them. Have you ever been in that situation? Sometimes we struggle to identify someone from their voice alone. Here Jesus describes sheep that have no such problem: they can easily identify the voice of their shepherd.

1 How do you think these sheep learnt to identify their shepherd's voice?

2 What are the benefits of following the right shepherd?

3 Are you following Jesus, the good shepherd or do you sometimes find yourself listening to other voices?

4 How can we make sure we are always following Jesus and not someone else?

3 Sharing Jesus

Speaking about Jesus, witnessing and evangelism: for some of us these things will be exciting, challenging, a reason to live. For others they may bring feelings of fear or embarrassment or failure. We may have bad experiences of people sharing Jesus with us or have seen angry or confused reactions from others. More positively we may remember the words used by people who brought us to Jesus with affection and gratitude. We may be quick-thinking extroverts for whom any chance to speak about Jesus is a joy; we may be shy introverts who can't put a sentence together without tripping up in the middle. We are all going to approach the idea of speaking about our faith differently, but there is no doubt that we are all called to play an active part in sharing Jesus with the lost world around us.

Setting Out

1 What mental picture do you have when you hear someone described as an evangelist?

2 Would you describe your response as positive or negative? Why?

3 Your small group meeting starts up and the leader asks people to share experiences of speaking about their faith to someone. Would you be most likely to:

    a Make an excuse and leave – you're terrified by the whole idea of sharing your faith;

    b Hide and hope you don't get picked on – you can't remember when you last spoke to someone about Jesus;

    c Open the discussion – you've had several great conversations this week;

    d Divert things by discussing how awful the street evangelist was in town last Saturday;

    e Offer a few not very successful experiences from quite a while ago;

    f Share that good conversation you had the other week;

    g Argue that the whole discussion is pointless – living like Jesus is far more important than talking about it.

4 How does the idea that you might speak to someone about Jesus make you feel? Why?

5 Have you seen this done in a way that you felt was unhelpful for those listening? If so, what made it so?

6 Have you seen someone speaking effectively about Jesus? What made the difference?

Signposts

Read John 4:1–42.

Jesus arrives tired, hungry and thirsty at the Samaritan village of Sychar. The Samaritans did not have a good relationship with the Jews. Their enmity stretched back to the destruction of Israel by Assyria (2 Kings 17:6) and the subsequent intermarriage of the Jewish remnant with the incomers. Not only that, the person that approached the well was a woman on her own. Any Jewish male concerned about his reputation and purity wouldn't dream of speaking to a woman in such circumstances; just notice how stunned the disciples were on their return (v 27).

1 Jesus asks the woman for a drink. Why do you think he started the conversation this way, rather than going straight to talking about her relationships?

Jesus wants the woman to know who he is and what that means for her. Even so he lets her misunderstand and raise theological red herrings before an opportunity to tell her he is the Messiah arises.

2 How do you think the conversation would have gone if Jesus had told her who he was much sooner?

3 What do you think Jesus' conversation with the woman tells us about his attitude towards her?

4 Imagine the woman hadn't been feeling chatty that day. What do you think would have happened? Why?

ORDINARY EVENTS

An ordinary task leads to the transformation of the Samaritan woman and the lives of a whole village forever. We all spend much of our time doing ordinary routine tasks.

1 Do we look for God to use us in ordinary activities as well as in the more obvious ways, such as in church ministry?

2 Not all our everyday activities involve speaking to others. Is it possible for God to use these tasks to share the message of Jesus too?

Fred and Bob do jobs they don't really enjoy. They are both looking forward to the end of their shift, when they will go and serve in the local homeless shelter. Fred sees his time at work as just something to get through, a means of making enough money to do his real work for God at the shelter. Bob on the other hand believes he can serve God at work as well. He prays for the people he meets, looks for opportunities to care for them and just occasionally gets a chance to talk about Jesus.

3 When you think about your work (paid or unpaid, inside or outside the home), do you think you are more like Fred or Bob?

4 Do you think God's desire or ability to use us at work is affected by what our job is?

5 How could someone in an 'ordinary' job or one they don't enjoy make that a place they serve God?

SERVING WITH EXCITEMENT

At this point the story separates into two strands. One strand sees the woman spreading the news about Jesus to her village and the other sees Jesus talking to the disciples.

1 Many of us will have experienced a time when our feelings affected our desire to eat. Grief, excitement, anger, worry, fear – all of these things can make us want to react by eating more or not eating at all. Can you think of a time this was true for you? Why is this?

2 What do you think Jesus was feeling here that meant he wasn't hungry anymore?

3 Why do you think he was feeling this way?

4 Have you ever experienced a time when serving God made you feel as good as Jesus obviously did here? If so, what was it about that experience that made you feel that way?

5 Such a positive reaction to an experience of serving God may be an indication that this is an area we are especially gifted for or called to. Why might our feelings be such a clue?

6 How else might someone know that they are called to a particular area or type of ministry?

7 What if you never feel this way after serving God? Does that mean you shouldn't bother doing it?

8 Many people feel unsure about how God wants to use them. Do you think that is true for you? If so, what areas of ministry or service have you tried out?

9 When we try new things, sometimes we realise we're in the wrong job after all. Have you had that experience? How did you react to that?

10 When you look back over such experiences of ministry or serving others, were there some things you enjoyed about them? What bad things were there? What could you learn from these experiences that might help you identify a new area of ministry to try?

REAPING THE HARVEST

1 Jesus describes the people who don't know him as the ripening fields ready for the harvest, and us as the harvesters. Does that mean we should be seeking to turn every conversation we have round to God? Is it our duty for example to share a Bible verse with the checkout operator or bring Jesus into every conversation we have with our friends? Why do you say that?

2 Jesus built a connection with the woman that eventually changed her life. What could we learn from this event to help us as we try to share Jesus with others?

Prayer

All of us have had people who shared their experience of Jesus with us. We may have been brought up in a Christian family or been active in Sunday schools or other kinds of children's and youth work. We may have heard about Jesus first from a friend or through coming to church or an event much later in life.

Spend a few minutes thinking of the people who were instrumental in bringing you to faith in Jesus and then those who have helped you nurture and grow that relationship.

Q: What would your life be like if they had not done that?

If you meet with a group, either pray silently together or share one sentence prayers of thanks for these people and their contribution to your lives.

Then continue to pray together for those people you know who don't follow Jesus. Think about the ways their lives would change if they had a growing relationship with him. Pray for each person by name, including praying for their needs and concerns from everyday life. Ask God to give you an opportunity to share something of Jesus with them this week. If you meet with a group you might like to share any encouraging conversations you have been able to have with those you are particularly praying for.

Further Afield

1 TELLING MY STORY

'. . . and if you are asked about your Christian hope, always be ready to explain it.' 1 Peter 3:15b

Read Acts 22:1–23 and 2 Corinthians 1:8–11.

1 In the first passage Paul describes how he came to faith in Jesus; the second tells of God working in his life more recently. If you were asked to tell the story of how you first came to faith, what would you say? Why did you choose to follow Jesus?

2 If you were asked to say what God is doing for you today what would you say then? What difference is he making to your life now?

3 Spend some time considering what you would say in these two situations. Are you ready to explain what God has done – and is doing – in your life, if someone asks?

If you are meeting with a group, why not give people a chance to share their answers to one or both questions? It's a great way to practise speaking about what God is doing in your life and to encourage one another with the answers.

2 GOD'S FREE GIFT

Read John 6.

Many items in a newsagent or supermarket come with a free item. Do these things make you more likely to buy it? Whether you do or not, presumably they do increase sales. People like freebies! In John 6 we see the crowd following

Jesus getting an unexpected free meal. The next day what happens? More people turn up, drawn by the possibility of free food. Jesus reminds them that following him is not just about getting good things today, but has eternal significance.

Do you ever find yourself expecting following Jesus to bring you good things? Maybe you hope for new relationships, a role in life, material possessions or help from other Christians? Here we are reminded that we should follow him whatever life brings us; HE is all that matters.

John says that by the end of that day 'many of his disciples had turned away and deserted'. Even amongst the believers many gave up because it all seemed less simple than they had thought. If faith is based only on the hope of rewards from God it isn't going to survive when challenges come.

Spend some time appreciating the gift of God himself. Maybe you could write some words or phrases that describe his character or just look out of a window and appreciate his creation around you. Pray that whatever happens in life, your relationship with him will always be enough for you.

3 RIGHTEOUS ANGER

Read John 2:13–17.

The temple was filled with people unfairly profiteering from the needs of the ordinary people. Jesus gets angry – this house of worship, and the worshippers themselves, are suffering harm. Do we get angry over the social injustices we see around us? Do we do anything about them? Do we even notice?

Pray that this week God will help you notice injustices around you. Sometimes these are so big it seems impossible for us to make any difference at all, but if nobody acts, nothing will change. Consider how you could make a difference to just one person or situation this week. If you meet as a group, perhaps you could share your ideas together and then choose one or more to put into action.

4 The Way we Live

Did you ever admire someone so much that you wanted to be just like them? If so, perhaps you changed your hair or your clothes to match theirs. Maybe you tried to copy the way they walked or that distinctive flick of their hair. Perhaps you spent hours trying to imitate their style of taking free kicks or playing the guitar. Perhaps you still do; after all many adults show allegiance to their team, band or hobby in some way. Whether we think this way or not, as followers of Jesus we have the greatest hero of them all to admire. Jesus describes himself as 'an example to follow' (John 13:15) and we are called to put all our energies into being just like him.

Setting Out

1 Rebel or Rule-keeper – which of these is most like you?

A Rebel:

- Liked to personalise their uniform a little at school;
- Ignores direction signs in a car park if it makes it easier to get to that empty space;
- Sees a sign saying 'don't walk on the grass' and walks on it even when they don't really want to.

A Rule keeper:

- Wouldn't have dreamt of wearing anything but the exact uniform requirements;
- Would drive half a mile round the empty car park to get to a particular space if that's what the signs said;
- Would go out of their way to check that they were allowed to walk on any grass before doing so.

Which is most like you? Why do you react that way?

2 Can you think of other times when someone might want to 'stretch' the rules a little?

3 Are some rules made to be broken?

Signposts

THREE MARKS OF THE FOLLOWER

1 Obedience

Read John 14:15–26 and 1 Peter 1:14–16.

1 Why might someone obey a rule?

2 Why might someone obey Jesus?

3 Do you think obeying Jesus is about keeping his rules or not? Why?

4 Does being obedient to Jesus mean giving up our individuality?

5 Imagine you've been asked to make yourself into a celebrity lookalike. With the company's technology you can look like anyone at all. Who would you choose to look like?

6 What do you think would make someone a successful lookalike?

7 Being like Jesus isn't about looking like him, but about having an internal makeover so we are like him in character. Do you think having the physical Jesus with us, like the disciples, would make this easier? Why?

8 Even though Jesus isn't here in person, he didn't leave us to our own devices as we try to live like him. Here John tells us that we have the Holy Spirit at work in us. How does he help us to be like Jesus?

9 We all get things wrong and sometimes fail to be much like Jesus at all. At other times wrong patterns of behaviour take root in our lives even when we

know that isn't what God wants for us. Is that true in your life at the moment? If so, how can you begin to change that?

10 Sometimes it can be very hard to change such established behaviour. If you need to do that is there a trusted friend who could support you? Or could you ask your group to encourage you and pray for you, even if you don't feel able to explain all the details? Is there other help you could seek out?

2 Bearing Fruit

Read John 15:1–8.

The image of the vine to represent Israel is a long-standing idea (e.g. Jeremiah 2:20–22 and Psalm 80:8–16). Here Jesus says he is the true vine, the true Israel. He is the one who will be able to bring people to know God.

1 The following passages describe different kinds of fruit we are looking to produce as followers of Jesus:

    a John 4:36;
    b Romans 7:4;
    c Galatians 5:22,23.

Which of these do you think matters most? Why?

2 Is your life bearing fruit in these ways today?

Read 1 Corinthians 3:10–15.

Paul makes it clear that one day our work (the fruit of our lives) will be tested.

1 What decides whether that work has value or is to be destroyed? (You may want to look at John 15:4–6.)

2 We are warned to build our lives on Jesus, but what other foundations might we build on instead? (Matthew 6:1–4 might be helpful here.)

Basil is a Christian and has spent his whole life working with the poor. Many people have benefited enormously from his efforts. Basil could have done this because God called him to and he wanted to serve him. However, really Basil chose it so that other people would think well of him (and they do).

3 Do you think God really cares what made Basil get involved in such work? After all it has been highly successful – doesn't that mean God was pleased with him?

4 What might it mean for a life's work such as Basil's to be destroyed?

5 How could Basil have made sure that his life and work was built on the one sure foundation: Jesus?

6 Are you really building your life on Jesus?

3 Living in Love

Read John 13:1–17.

1 Jesus washing the disciples feet was completely unexpected. Why did he do it?

2 We don't welcome people into our homes by washing their feet. How might Jesus have demonstrated his love for the disciples today?

3 How might we express such servant love to others?

LOVE FOR ONE ANOTHER

Read John 13:33–35 and 1 John 3:11–18.

1 (Without naming names!) Does anyone in your church (or small group) ever:
   a Get annoyed with someone;
   b Ignore someone who is different from them or not in 'their group';
   c Speak abruptly;

d Promise to ring or visit someone when they are ill and then not do it;

e Moan about something someone else did wrong;

f Resent someone muscling in on what they see as their territory or task;

g Gossip?

2 When you look at Jesus' relationships, what characteristics mark them out?

3 Why does it matter what our relationships with others in our church are like?

4 Where are the relationships in your church (or this small group) strong? What are you good at? And where are they weak? What do you need to work on?

5 What about you? What do you see in Jesus' relationships that you find hard to put into practice in your own?

6 Is there a particular relationship that you are having difficulty with at the moment? What could you do to try and put things right? How could your group pray for you?

AN EXAMPLE TO FOLLOW

I have given you an example to follow. Do as I have done to you. John 13:15

1 Why do you think it matters what kind of person we are?

2 Jesus said we were to 'make disciples' (Matthew 28:19). We can see easily how what we say or do is important in doing that. How can our character, the kind of person we are, help too?

3 As Christians our character and lifestyle show others what following Jesus means and how it makes a difference. What do others really learn from you?

Prayer

For each section, begin by reading the verses from Philippians and then the following suggestion for reflection. Allow a few minutes for people either to pray silently or aloud, before ending each section by saying the words in bold together.

1 OUR CHURCH

Is there any encouragement from belonging to Christ? Any comfort from his love? Any fellowship together in the Spirit? Are your hearts tender and sympathetic? Then make me truly happy by agreeing wholeheartedly with each other, loving one another, and working together with one heart and purpose. Philippians 2:1,2

Q: Do the relationships in your church match Paul's hopes for the Philippians?

Give thanks for the positive things you see in these relationships.

Lord, we pray for our church. You place us in this community to live together as your people. Help our relationships to grow and deepen as we follow Jesus together.

2 IT BEGINS WITH ME

Don't be selfish; don't live to make a good impression on others. Be humble, thinking of others as better than yourself. Don't think only about your own affairs, but be interested in others, too, and what they are doing. Your attitude should be the same that Christ Jesus had. Philippians 2:3–5

I always need to be the first person willing to change. Ask God to show you where you need to become more like him in your relationships.

Lord, I don't always behave well in my relationships. Show me how to love people more effectively and help me have the courage to change when necessary.

3 SACRIFICIAL LOVE

Though he was God, he did not demand and cling to his rights as God. He made himself nothing; he took the humble position of a slave and appeared in human form. And in human form he obediently humbled himself even further by dying a criminal's death on a cross. Philippians 2:6–8

Jesus showed us what sacrificial love is all about. Thank him for what he has done for you

Lord may we live lives that are marked by a sacrificial, servant love for others.

4 'So that . . . every tongue will confess'

Because of this, God raised him up to the heights of heaven and gave him a name that is above every other name, so that at the name of Jesus every knee will bow, in heaven and on earth and under the earth, and every tongue will confess that Jesus Christ is Lord, to the glory of God the Father. Philippians 2:9–11

We are called to live in love so that others will know Jesus. End by praying together for those people you know who don't yet follow Jesus.

Lord, this week, help us to demonstrate how much you love those who don't yet follow you.

Further Afield

1 PRUNING

Read John 15:1–8.

Did you ever find yourself with two choices but not liking either? Whether it is trivial or a much bigger issue in life, we probably wish we could add a third, more palatable, alternative. As we read that branches of the vine will either be cut off or pruned we may feel the same way here too, and yet we are only pruned if it will be worth it in the end. God uses even the most painful events to help us serve him more effectively.

1　What do you think it means for a person to be pruned?

Difficulties and challenges can be things to endure before we get on with life again, or opportunities to learn from God however much we may long for them to end.

2　Are you facing particular challenges at the moment? However difficult your circumstances, pray that God would use them to help you grow.

2 REAL JOY

Read John 15:1–11.

When was the last time you felt so excited that it burst out of you? Sometimes it's impossible to keep good news a secret. Bad news can mark us too: we behave differently, respond differently and our body language changes. Even when people don't know us they'll be able to tell which kind of news we have received. Jesus promises that his love will fill us with overflowing joy, but such joy isn't the same as happy feelings bubbling out of us. Joy is the unchanging certainty of God's love and presence in our lives, something that underpins every up and down we meet.

When have you experienced very different feelings about events in your life? Did your relationship with God change depending on how you were feeling? If so, how?

Ask God to help you know the certainty of his presence and love however you feel.

3. LOVE YOUR ENEMIES

Read Matthew 5:43–48 and John 15:12.

Enemies fight on opposite sides in a war, tease you in the playground and wish you harm. Even if we don't feel we have any enemies, do we feel warmly towards everyone? What about the person who carves us up on the road; our colleague who grabs the glory at work; or the irritating neighbour whose TV is always too loud?

1 If you were in one of these situations, what would you be praying for?

2 How could someone show love to the annoying other person in these situations?

3 Is there someone whose actions hurt or annoy you. How could you show love to that person?

Sometimes we are so hurt by someone's actions that the last thing we want is for them to experience anything good at all. If that is true for you, begin by asking God to help you want to change. Otherwise pray for someone you find difficult or demanding. Ask God how you can show his love to them today.

5 *Making an Impact*

*H*ave you ever had the experience of seeing something so often that you no longer even notice it? Then one day something draws it to your attention again. Maybe it's changed in some way – perhaps a new poster has gone up or the building has been repainted. Maybe someone points it out to you and now it's as though you've seen the crack in the basin or the dust under the chair for the first time. Now you can't stop noticing it!

In our society Jesus is a name that many people find very familiar. They think they know who he is and what his Church is all about. In fact he may seem so familiar and yet often so unimportant that they go through life without really noticing him at all. As Christians we need to introduce people to Jesus in such a way that it is as though they are hearing about him for the very first time.

Setting Out

1 How good are you at doing two things at once? Try singing a song and clapping at the same time. Can you do it?

2 Now sing again but this time also write down the alphabet backwards, or the 17-times-table, whilst you're singing (no cheating!). Did you manage to do both tasks properly? Why?

If your group doesn't like singing then try reading a Bible passage or a poem together instead.

3 It is often suggested that men can't do more than one thing at once, whereas women are good at multi-tasking. Do you think this is really true?

4 What about you, do you fit that pattern or not?

5 How much do the tasks themselves affect our ability to do two or more things at once?

6 Is it fair to say that to do our best with a task we must give it our full attention?

Signposts

All of us have many things trying to occupy our attention. If you see a trailer for a new TV series or a film at the cinema, what makes you decide whether to watch it or not?

We probably ignore much of the advertising we see for programmes, films, books, bands and magazines, perhaps in part because we don't expect these things to be interesting or relevant to us. When we want to introduce people to Jesus we may face similar problems to these advertisers. People often have impressions of the Church and of Christians which mean they don't expect our message, even Jesus himself, to have anything to offer them. We need to encourage people to give Jesus unprejudiced attention.

1 SURPRISE!

Read John 2:1–12, 3:1,2 and John 4:5–10.

What made these people take an interest in Jesus:

a The guests at the wedding at Cana;
b Nicodemus;
c The Samaritan woman?

Read John 4:39–42, Acts 2:43–47, Acts 9:33–35.

You don't have to meet Jesus in the flesh to be intrigued by him. What raised these people's interest:

a The villagers of Sychar;
b Those being added to the group daily;
c The population of Lydda and Sharon?

2 WHAT ABOUT TODAY?

What people believe about Jesus

1 Who do you think people in our society believe Jesus is or was?

2 Do you think a person's age makes any difference to the beliefs they hold about Jesus?

3 What else might influence the ideas someone has about Jesus?

4 Why do you think some people hold ideas about Jesus that are different from those we see in the Bible?

5 Does it matter what people outside the Church believe about Jesus?

What people believe about the Church

1 Today many people's only contact with the Church is through TV or newspapers. What might they think about the Church as a result of the media? What would they say we are all about?

2 Do you think the impression of the Church given by the media is deserved or accurate? Why?

3 What about your local press? Does that treat the Church any differently?

Making an Impression

Many non-Christians have no Christian friends and have never been in a church. They aren't likely to think about Jesus, Christians or the Church and would see these things as irrelevant to them.

1 How can a church make an impact on such a person? Should we bother trying?

2 What impression of your church and its concerns do you think people living nearby have?

3 What difference would it make to non-Christians living near your church if it shut down?

4 Would it make a difference if you exclude community activities that take place at your church, or services you offer the community such as weddings, a playgroup or a hall to hire?

5 What about the people who don't come near a church. Does your church go out into the community to reach such people?

If not, how might a church do this?

3 CREATING A CONNECTION

Four people are reading the same book. One hates it. One thinks it's ok but a bit slushy. One cries through most of it but loves it. One finds it boring.

What might lie behind such different responses to the same story?

Read John 9.

1 How did the following people respond to the blind man's healing:
   a The Pharisees;
   b The blind man himself;
   c The man's parents;
   d His neighbours?

2 What lay behind their very different responses to this one event?

Our interests and experiences, needs and hopes and fears all affect the way we respond to something. Everyone's life history and personality is different and yet as Christians we still believe that Jesus is the answer for us all, bringing us salvation, reconciliation with God and hope for the future. Today people may be more willing to hear our message if we demonstrate how Jesus can make a difference to the needs and hopes of their daily life. Some may need comfort or help to change when their lives are falling apart. Some may be looking for truth or purpose in life. Others may want to live life well and be looking for a model to follow. We can't presume people will make such connections for themselves; we have to go out and show them why Jesus is the answer for them too.

3   Do you agree that we should deliberately try to show people how Jesus can make a difference in their life?

4   Do you think it is still important to tell people that they are sinners in need of salvation from Jesus?

5   If you had time to tell someone only one thing about Jesus what would it be and why?

6   A member of your church brings a along a visitor to your main time of corporate worship. What one thing do you think they would remember about the:
    a   Atmosphere;
    b   Welcome;
    c   Facilities;
    d   Worship;
    e   Teaching?

7   Do you think your church would have surprised them in some (positive) way? If you asked them what one thing they had learnt about Jesus that they didn't know before, what do you think it would be?

8   Do you think the experience of attending worship at your church would encourage them to investigate Jesus further? Why?

9   Is that something you see happening at your church at the moment? For example, do non-Christians come along? If so, do they keep coming? Do they go on to become followers of Jesus themselves?

10 If this process does happen at your church, what makes it work? Does it rely on the efforts of a few or is everyone involved in some way?

11 If this isn't happening where does the process break down? Why is that? For example, is it that the only new people are Christians already? Is it that non-Christians do come but never become regulars?

12 What about you, what part do you play in seeing people become followers of Jesus?

Prayer

The aim of this session is to pray for your local community.

You might like to consider the following.

- What the significant buildings and places are in your area. What do these offer to your area? How could you pray for these places and their impact on your community?
- What other needs does your area have?
- What good things can you give thanks for?

You might find local newspapers, photos or a map of the area useful.

Some groups might like to spend this time walking around the area, praying for people and places as you go.

Also pray for the events and activities that connect your church to your community, both those that take place on your premises and those that take place out in the locality. Pray for all those involved.

Finally pray again for your relationships with people who don't yet know Jesus and also for any particular needs those people have at present.

Further Afield

1 MIXED RESPONSES

Read John 11:1–53.

1 It's hard to imagine anyone being disappointed by Jesus' arrival but Martha was. Lazarus was dead and Jesus had come. Why didn't she respond to Jesus more positively?

2 Lazarus is brought back to life, an experience that must have stunned those watching. Why do you think some people responded so negatively?

3 For some, even this amazing miracle wasn't enough to see them put their trust in Jesus. Whatever we do or say some people will decide not to follow Jesus. Does that mean that if someone responds negatively we should give up trying to convince them of the good news of Jesus?

4 Who do you know that seems impervious to the good news of Jesus? How could you pray for them today?

2 GOD'S POWER ALONE

Read 1 Corinthians 2:1–5 and 3:7–9.

Given a fantastic new product to promote we'd expect any advertising company to come up with a hard-hitting campaign, not to keep things low-key. Paul however didn't use dramatic methods to sell his message about Jesus, but kept his words 'very plain'.

Why do you think Paul chose to use such a low-key style of preaching? Was it just because he was nervous?

Paul knew that his listeners weren't convinced by his wonderful speeches but by God alone. Like Paul, we are called to share Jesus with others, to take our opportunities and live as light in the world. Even so, we always know that God is ultimately responsible for the outcome. Of course, we are still to do our best and avoid unnecessary mistakes, but ultimately it is God's power that makes things happen, not us.

2 In serving God, when do you rely too much on your own abilities?

3 How often do you begin by asking God to show you how he wants you to speak or act? Where do you particularly need to do that at the moment?

4 How do you respond when something goes well? Do you give God the glory or prefer to seek praise for yourself?

3 LOVE, LOVE, LOVE

Read Luke 18:9–14.

The Pharisee's good deeds are fatally undermined by what is in his heart. We are all saved only by God's grace and mercy. How would you sum up your attitude to those around you who don't yet know Jesus? Are you ever at risk of feeling superior to them in some way.

Spend a few moments reflecting on your imperfections. Ask God for his forgiveness and thank him for the mercy he shows you.

Now Read Ephesians 5:2.

Sometimes it isn't easy to love other people and that can come across in the way we think about them or respond to them.

Who do you find hard to love? Do you think they realise that from the way you are with them? Or does it affect your attitude to them? How can you demonstrate God's love to them?

Pray that God would help you show his love to all those in your life.

6 *Final Destination*

hether you look back to a single moment when you made the decision to follow Jesus, or whether it was a slow and steady process, that wasn't an ending of an old life but a new beginning in your journey with Jesus. As Christians we want to bring others to make that decision too but that isn't our only concern. Walking with Jesus is a life-long commitment, a process that gives meaning and purpose for every day. We need to encourage people to become disciples: people who are growing more like Jesus and whose faith makes a difference every day; people who are light in a dark world.

Setting Out

1 You've decided it's time you learnt to play a musical instrument. Do you:

   a Go and get all the gear, then get bored after two lessons;
   b Get started and love it until it gets hard and you really do have to work at it;
   c Find yourself, two years later, in the local band and having a great time;
   d Wake up the next morning, decide this was a daft idea and forget it?

2 You're going on holiday and it's going to be a long journey. Do you:

   a Plan your route with great care to make sure it's as short as possible;
   b Just set off – you know the way roughly so you're sure it will be fine;
   c Set off on your planned route, see something interesting on the way and go off to investigate it, and arrive at your destination very late;
   d Pay someone else to drive you and sleep all the way?

3 You've got something to do for work on Monday. Do you:

   a Come home on Friday and get on with it immediately – you'd like it out of the way;
   b Do it really late on Sunday evening – you never miss a deadline but it can get close!
   c Keep getting it out but then find other jobs you must do first such as the shopping, the gardening or polishing the cat;
   d Give up and not bother with it – you'll just have to apologise on Monday?

4 Are you someone who gets distracted easily? Or can you spend hours and hours on a single project (or even months and months)?

5 How much does your interest in what you are doing make a difference to your answer?

6 What else might affect our enthusiasm and commitment to a task?

7 Does it matter what we are like? Why?

Signposts

DECIDING TO COMMIT

Read John 3:1–21, John 7:37–52 and John 19:38–42.

1 How does Nicodemus' attitude to Jesus change over the course of these three passages?

2 Nicodemus had obviously been impressed by Jesus. Why do you think this first, private meeting didn't end with Nicodemus going public as a follower of Jesus?

Even Jesus didn't see everyone come to instant faith in him. Developing faith is often a process just as it was for Nicodemus. Maybe you can see how that was true in your life or the life of someone else you know. However, sometimes people don't complete the process at all.

Read Matthew 19:16–22.

1 We don't know whether this young man ever changed his mind. What was it that put him off following Jesus at this time?

2 Do you think Jesus should have made fewer demands on the man to keep him interested? Why?

3 Is it possible to try too hard to get someone to follow Jesus?

4 What if people come to our church, hear the good news of Jesus and then decide they don't want to follow him? Does this mean we've done something wrong somewhere?

THE COST OF COMMITMENT

Read John 15:18 – 16:4.

1 What did Jesus say would happen to his followers?

2 Jesus didn't pretend that everything would run smoothly. Why do you think he gave the disciples advance warning of the troubles coming their way?

3 Do you think there are still costs involved in following Jesus in our society?

4 If so, do we need to spell them out to someone before they decide to follow Jesus?

MISSION ACCOMPLISHED?

We've got their attention, shown them how Jesus can change their life, warned them of the potential cost of following him . . . and they've made that decision to serve him. They're saved and they're coming to church. They're done. Next! But we can't stop there. We are to bring people into that new relationship with Jesus and then to help them become disciples, people transformed by Jesus.

Read Matthew 28:19,20.

1 Jesus calls us to make disciples. What's the difference between making converts and making disciples?

2 Why is it important that a person who decides to follow Jesus goes on to become a disciple?

FOUR MARKS OF A DISCIPLE

1 We put Jesus first

Yes, a person is a fool to store up earthly wealth but not have a rich relationship with God. Luke 12:21

Going to church or a small group, being involved in ministry or reading the Bible every day don't automatically guarantee that someone is growing as a disciple. It is perfectly possible to drift along surrounded by other Christians and doing 'Christian things' but neglecting our relationship with Jesus. God still loves us and wants to use us when we don't spend time with him alone, but that will make us slower to grow, not as effective, and less like Jesus than we could be.

Read Mark 1:35, Hebrews 4:12 and 2 Timothy 3:16.

1   What reasons for spending time alone with God do these verses give us?

2   How important is it for you to spend time alone with God? Do you enjoy this time?

3   What difference do you think it would make if you spent more time alone with God?

4   Are there things you find difficult about doing this? If so, what kind of help could your small group or your church offer you?

5   Do you want to be more like Jesus? Spending time alone with God is not about fulfilling an obligation, but about connecting with him, learning how to be like him and sharing the things on our heart with him.

2 We develop our character

Read 1 Samuel 16:7.

Being a disciple is more about what we are like, than what we do.

1   Why do you think God cares more about our character than our actions?

2   Does that mean we shouldn't be doing things for him?

3   What kind of characteristics does God want us to show?

4   What might help us develop these things in our lives?

3 We don't keep any part of life back from God

Read Romans 13:12–14.

1   Should being a Christian make any difference to someone in these situations? If so, how?

    a   You're going out to the cinema tonight. How do you choose your film?

    b   Unexpectedly you've been given £5000. What do you choose to spend it on?

    c   Someone at work has behaved badly and you are really annoyed with them. Usually your colleagues react with lots of moaning and making the culprit feel bad, perhaps by not including them in the coffee run or walking out of a room when they walk in.

2   Do you think you really do behave differently because of your faith or not?

3   What areas of your daily life are still to come under God's authority?

4 We are serving him

Read Romans 12:3–5 and 1 Corinthians 12:17.

1   Why is it important for us to serve?

2   We don't have to be a missionary or paid to work in a church to serve God. We all serve wherever God has placed us. How can we serve him through the routines of life?

3   How can a church encourage its members to serve Jesus?

FINALLY

Our relationships, our values, our choices – they all matter to God; Jesus is not just for Sundays!

1 How can a church develop its converts into disciples?

2 If we want to grow as a disciple, we need to realise it won't just happen automatically. We need to take responsibility for our own spiritual growth. How can we do that?

3 Are you willing to make the commitment in time and changed priorities for this to happen in your life?

Jesus calls us to make disciples, people who will take their turn in making disciples of others, people who will play their part in building his Church and bringing about God's purposes for the world.

Prayer

1 PRAISE

When I think of the wisdom and scope of God's plan, I fall to my knees and pray to the Father, the Creator of everything in heaven and on earth.
Ephesians 3:14,15

Begin with a time of praise. Ask people to come prepared to share either a verse that expresses praise or with a one-sentence prayer of praise.
If someone isn't confident enough to read or pray aloud, they can write down their contribution, and perhaps ask someone else to read it out.

After everyone has read their contributions spend a few moments in silence, reflecting on the glory of the Creator God.

2 PRAYER FOR ONE ANOTHER

Use the words from Ephesians 3:16–19 as a prayer.

If your group isn't too big, have someone read out these words as a prayer for each person in the group in turn, beginning each time with the person's name. Larger groups could split up into two or three smaller groups to do this.

Between each reading of the passage, spend a few moments praying together for that person before moving on.

If you are working through this book alone you could either insert your own name and pray for yourself, or use it to pray for someone else today.

Name, I pray that from his glorious, unlimited resources he will give you mighty inner strength through his Holy Spirit. And I pray that Christ will be more and more at home in your heart as you trust in him. May your roots go down deep into the soil of God's marvellous love. And may you have the power to understand, as all God's people should, how wide, how long, how high, and how deep his love really is. May you experience the love of Christ, though it is so great you will never fully understand it. Then you will be filled with the fullness of life and power that comes from God.

3 LOOKING OUTWARDS

Pray again for the people we know who don't yet follow Jesus, sharing any particular successes or needs.

4 FINALLY

End by reading these words from Ephesians 3:20,21 together:

Now glory be to God! By his mighty power at work within us, he is able to accomplish infinitely more than we would ever dare to ask or hope. May he be given glory in the church and in Christ Jesus forever and ever through endless ages. Amen.

Further Afield

1 DEVELOPING DISCIPLESHIP

Read 2 Peter 1:2–11.

There must be a great many of us whose favourite New Year's Resolution is never to make another resolution. We know ourselves too well! We know that we may set off with great enthusiasm but in a few days, maybe even only a few hours, we'll slip back into the old ways. Changing a bad habit is unlikely to be easy or happen overnight. We need lots of perseverance to bring about that better figure, the healthier lifestyle or finished project.

Here Peter reminds us that becoming like Jesus also requires perseverance. The good news is that there are great rewards and we can experience them now, as we become more like Jesus, and in eternity.

1 Do you see yourself as someone who is determined to grow more like Jesus whatever it takes?

2 Or do you find yourself giving up, someone who is easily discouraged?

If that's more like you, why not consider asking a friend or your small group to support you. Maybe you could meet up or if that's difficult then ring, email or text one another and share your struggles and successes on a regular basis.

2 FINISHING THE RACE

Read 2 Timothy 4:6–8.

We've all heard the story of the hare and the tortoise. For most of the race the hare is well ahead but then overconfidence means he feels able to stop midrace for a nap. Meanwhile the tortoise has stayed focused on the race and ends up winning. As Christians we are called to be like the tortoise! We aren't looking to crawl through life, but to be people who keep focused on the end of the race, not allowing ourselves to get distracted or give up.

Here Paul looks back over his life and is able to say that he has lived a life that brought honour to God – that was focused on serving him right to the end.

1 One day do you want to be able to look back over your life and say these words with Paul? What might pull you off course?

2 What can you do to help yourself stay focused on the end of the race?

3 GOD AT WORK IN THE WORLD

Read Isaiah 40:9–31.

Reflect on this passage from Isaiah. What does God want to say to you today?

Praise him for his power and glory as our Creator God who also loves and cherishes his people.

End by waiting on him, seeking his strength to serve him today.

To whet your appetite for more of Kate's books, the next seven pages contain a sample chapter from one of her earlier studies, *The Journey of the Son*.

Hope in the darkness

Have you ever chosen to spend the night out of doors, or do you like the comfort of a mattress and sheets too much to even consider it? It is said that the darkest hour is just before the dawn; that when the darkness seems to be completely impenetrable that's really the moment when the first streaks of dawn light appear in the sky.

In this session we come to the moment in history when it seemed that this time the dawn would not appear, that the darkness had really won at last. For a short time, the death of Jesus appeared to be the end, the victory going to the powers of darkness, the Son of God defeated. With hindsight we know that wasn't so, but even here, as we focus on Good Friday, we can see glimmers of hope, reminders that in the darkest moments of our lives the light of God's power and love still shines on.

Setting Out

Optimist or pessimist – is your glass half-full or half-empty?

How would you respond in these situations?

1 The nightmare comes true. The exam's today and you've forgotten to do any preparation. Do you:

  a Stay in bed. You've no chance of passing so why bother turning up?
  b Leap out of bed and give it a go. What have you got to lose?
  c Something else?

2 You enter a competition to win tickets for something you'd really like to see. Do you:

  a Make a hotel booking as soon as you've posted the entry. How can you lose?
  b Buy your own tickets? You'll never win.
  c Something else?

3 You're walking towards the supermarket tills and all the queues are long. Do you:

  a Check exactly how much people have in their trolleys so you can choose the quickest queue?
  b Take the first queue you come to? It won't make any difference, you always get it wrong.
  c Something else?

4 You look out of the window. The sky is grey and the ground is damp but there's a tiny patch of blue directly above you. Do you:

    a Put on your raincoat and wellies and grab your umbrella? It's just the calm before the storm.

    b Put away your umbrella and make sure you've got your sunglasses handy? It's brightening up.

    c Something else?

Q: What do you think are the advantages of approaching life as an optimist? And a pessimist?

Q: Are there downsides to these approaches too? If so, what?

Q: Which are you most likely to be? Why do you think that is?

Signposts

Read

Matthew 20:17–19 and John 12:32–34

Q: How did the disciples and the crowd respond to the news that Jesus was going to die?

Q: Why do you think they didn't believe or understand him?

Q: Would it have made a difference if they had taken his message in? If so, how?

Even for the most naturally upbeat optimists among the disciples, it must surely have been impossible to foresee anything good coming from the events of Good Friday. As you read the following verses try to imagine what it was like for the disciples to live through that day without understanding what was going to happen next.

Read

Matthew 27:32–50

THREE MESSAGES OF HOPE

1 It's never too late

Q: How did people respond when they saw Jesus, who'd claimed to be the Son of God, dying on the cross (vs 39–43)?

Q: Why do you think they reacted like this?

Read

Matthew 27:44 and Luke 23:39–43

Q: Even the criminals mocked Jesus. What do you think made one of them later change sides?

That criminal made the decision to trust Jesus very late in life!

Q: Imagine two people. One makes that same decision early in life and follows Jesus, possibly even suffering for doing so, for many years. The other makes it just days before their death but receives the same forgiveness and promise of eternal life. Some might feel that this is unfair. Do you?

Q: Why do you think God allows this to happen? (You might find Romans 5:8 and Ephesians 2:8 helpful.)

Q: Imagine someone else then said, 'Well if that's the case I'll eat, drink and be merry and then repent (much) later on in life.' Maybe you hold that view yourself or know someone who does. What makes it worth following Jesus now instead of waiting?

Q: Have you made the decision to follow Jesus? If so, why did you decide to take the plunge when you did? If not, what is stopping you?

2 God never abandons us

Less than 24 hours after the Last Supper, Jesus was dead.

Q: How do you think the disciples felt about the three years they'd just spent following Jesus?

Q: How about the future? How do you think they felt about that?

Q: How can we be sure that, despite appearances, God was still in control of events here?

Q: In this darkest of moments, it must have seemed to the disciples as though everything was over, their dreams and hopes had been permanently shattered. We too can face times when it seems that we have been wasting our time following Jesus, that he has abandoned us. Have you ever felt like that?

Q: If so, and if that experience is now in the past, what brought you through it?

Q: What does the Bible promise us in times of disappointment and darkness? Read Isaiah 43:1,2 and Jeremiah 29:11.

Q: How could the experiences of the disciples here encourage us when we face tough situations?

3 Death is not the end

Read
Psalm 22:1–18 and Matthew 27:46

As Jesus took on the sins of the world on the cross, he experienced something that was even worse than the physical suffering – rejection by God. He cries out with words from Psalm 22:1: 'My God, my God, why have you forsaken me?'

Q: Many Psalms describe feelings of separation from God. Why do you think Jesus chose to quote from this one in particular?

Read

Psalm 22:19–31

Q: The suffering and separation described in the Psalm aren't all it has to say. What do these verses from the end of the Psalm promise God's people?

At the darkest hour of Jesus' life he quotes from a Psalm that points to God's promises for the future, to the hope that lies beyond suffering and death.

Prayer

Groups should begin by choosing someone to read the Bible passages. After each one, everyone may read the response together then pray in silence, using the suggestions.

Reader: 'In the beginning the Word already existed. He was with God, and he was God. He was in the beginning with God. He created everything there is. Nothing exists that he didn't make. Life itself was in him, and this life gives light to everyone. The light shines through the darkness, and the darkness can never extinguish it.'

John 1:1–5.

Response: Lord, you are the Creator God, the source of all life.

Think about the last few days. Where have you seen or experienced God's creation in that time? What do these things show you about God's character, what he is like? Praise him for these things.

Reader: 'But he was wounded and crushed for our sins. He was beaten that we might have peace. He was whipped, and we were healed!' Isaiah 53:5.

Response: Lord, you are the Sinless One, who chose to bear the punishment for our sin.

Again reflect on the last few days. What have you done that was wrong? Perhaps it was a one-off, a weak moment. Perhaps it's part of a pattern and you keep on making the same wrong choice. Remember that those things sent Jesus to the cross for you. Ask God to forgive you and give you a new start. Reflect on what you could do to make amends for your actions.

Reader: 'That is why we have a great High Priest who has gone to heaven, Jesus the Son of God. Let us cling to him and never stop trusting him. This High Priest of ours understands our weaknesses, for he faced all the same temptations we do, yet he did not sin. So let us come boldly to the throne of our gracious God. There we will receive his mercy, and we will find grace to help us when we need it.' Hebrews 4:14–16.

Response: Lord, you are the Servant King, the one who truly understands what it is like to be me.

As a man, Jesus knew what it was like to suffer; he experienced hunger, pain and injustice. He knew grief and fear, betrayal and death.

Think about yourself and those you love. Who is suffering or facing trouble at the moment?

What help do they need?

Pray for them, especially that they will experience the presence and the love of Jesus, the one who understands. Consider whether you could offer them any other support.

Further Afield

1 A KING'S WELCOME

Read

Philippians 2:1–11

Q: If you knew God's Son was about to arrive on earth, what kind of welcome would you expect him to receive?

Q: Why did Jesus give up the right to such a welcome?

Q: Are there times when we should give up our rightful expectations for the benefit of others? What might that mean for you at home; at work; at church?

2 OUR RESPONSE

Read

Psalm 19:14 and Matthew 16:24,25

The cross should change the way we live.

Q: What kind of life should a follower of Jesus be leading? Why?

Q: What are you finding most difficult to get right at the moment: words, thoughts or deeds? Why is that?

Q: What could you do to start the process of change in that area? Do you need to ask someone else for help or support?

Pray that God would help you to live your life in a way he considers worthy. Spend some time in silence, and allow him to point out where things are going well and not so well at the moment.

3 A RESPONSE OF PRAISE

Read

Psalm 145

Q: In praise, we celebrate God's character. What aspects of God's character does the writer describe in this Psalm?

'My mouth will speak in praise of the Lord' (v 21, NIV).

Whatever your composing skills, however long or short you want it to be, write your own psalm of praise to God. End by praying through that psalm.

OTHER TITLES by KATE HAYES

A Journey of the Heart: a pilgrim's guide to prayer

A companion to this book, with identical format. If you want to explore what it means to pray with purpose, growing in understanding of and intimacy with your God, this series of six Bible-based studies – which can be tackled in a small group or on your own – will take you on a rewarding journey. 48pp
ISBN 1 85999 797 X

The Journey of the Son

The second in this series of studies. Based on Matthew's portrayal of Jesus' road to the cross, these six studies consider the struggles we also face to do God's will. We see how Jesus coped with temptation and emotional turmoil, and stayed the course to the end. 48pp
ISBN 1 84427 097 1

A Journey of Discovery: on the road with Jesus' followers

Kate Hayes invites us to dig deeper into Luke's portrayal of how the first disciples grew in their understanding of Jesus and what it meant to be his disciples. What should be our priorities as we seek to live God's way? How can we cope with pressure and failure? 64pp
ISBN 1 84427 180 3

All suitable for individual or group use, at Lent or any other time.

THE RE:ACTION SERIES – 6 SMALL GROUP RESOURCES (all 48pp)

For the tough times
Does God care when I'm hurting?

Whether it's thousands killed in a terrorist attack as you watch on TV, your next door neighbour on chemo for cancer, or your best friend's marriage on shaky ground … there's no escaping the issue of suffering. Maybe you want to shout at God that's it's just so unfair! Just what's it all for?
ISBN 1 85999 622 1

Chosen for change
Am I part of God's big plan?

Like it or not, you're living in the 'me' culture. Are you comfortable with going it alone, taking care of 'Number One', cashing in on 'your rights' and turning a blind eye to responsibilities? What about sharing… caring… belonging… teamwork… community? Are you ready to serve not self – but society?
ISBN 1 85999 623 X

The possibility of purpose
What's the meaning of my life?
A treadmill existence of deadlines and pressures? Or a kaleidoscope of amazing opportunities? What's your take on daily life? Do you see yourself as a meaningless cosmic dust speck? Or a significant mover in a masterplan? Your view affects your motivation, your self-esteem, your priorities, your everyday choices…

ISBN 1 85999 620 5

Jesus: the sequel
Is he really coming back?
Appointments, schedules, timetables … we live in a time-bound society. It's so easy to live just for the present. Are you ready for the future? Not just your next career move… your next property… your next set of wheels… or even your plans for retirement. But the future that begins when Jesus himself returns!

ISBN 1 85999 621 3

More than fine words
Does my faith impact 24/7?
'Churchgoer' means 'hypocrite to many people. Yet Christians all agree that to show Jesus to others we need to people of integrity. Genuine. Real. Is that true of you? Does your day-to-day life reflect the reality of your beliefs? Do you 'walk the talk'? Is what you see, what you get?

ISBN 1 85999 770 8

More than bricks and ritual
Am I a team player for God?
Community is under threat. Contemporary lifestyles work against building relationships. Lives are increasingly independent and isolated. What of the Church? Does your life just briefly overlap with Christians on a Sunday morning? Are you missing out on God's vision for us as brothers and sisters? As a family? As a team?

ISBN 1 85999 769 4

Available from all good Christian bookshops or from Scripture Union Mail Order: PO Box 5148, Milton Keynes MLO, MK2 2YX, tel: 0845 0706006 or online through www.scriptureunion.org.uk

church@home
SU's online magazine for the world of small groups
www.scriptureunion.org.uk/churchathome
the one-stop shop for all your small group needs

SCRIPTURE UNION
USING THE BIBLE TO INSPIRE CHILDREN, YOUNG PEOPLE AND ADULTS TO KNOW GOD